ISO27001 / ISO27002

A Pocket Guide

Second edition

ISO27001 / ISO27002

A Pocket Guide

Second edition

ALAN CALDER

IT Governance Publishing

IT Governance Publishing
IT Governance Limited
Unit 3, Clive Court, Bartholomew's Walk
Cambridgeshire Business Park
Ely
Cambridgeshire
CB7 4EA
United Kingdom
www.itgovernance.co.uk

First published in the United Kingdom in 2008 by
IT Governance Publishing.

Second edition published in 2013.

ISBN 978-1-84928-522-3

FOREWORD

ISO/IEC 27001:2013 is the international Standard for Information Security Management Systems (ISMSs). Closely allied to ISO/IEC 27002:2013, this Standard (sometimes called the ISMS Standard) can help organisations meet all their information-related regulatory compliance objectives and can help them prepare and position themselves for new and emerging regulations.

Information is the lifeblood of today's organisation and, therefore, ensuring that information is simultaneously protected and available to those who need it is essential to modern business operations. Information systems are not usually designed from the outset to be secure. Technical security measures and checklists are limited in their ability to protect a complete information system. Management systems and procedural controls are essential components of any really secure information system and, to be effective, need careful planning and attention to detail.

ISO/IEC 27001 provides the specification for an ISMS and, in the related Code of Practice, ISO/IEC 27002, it draws on the knowledge of a group of experienced information security practitioners in a wide range of significant organisations across more than 40 countries to set out best practice in information security. An ISO27001-compliant system will provide a systematic approach to ensuring the availability, confidentiality and integrity of corporate information. The controls of ISO27001 are based on identifying and combating the entire range of potential risks to the organisation's information assets. This helpful, handy ISO27001/ISO27002 pocket guide gives a useful overview of these two important information security standards.

ABOUT THE AUTHOR

Alan Calder is a leading author on IT governance and information security issues. He is Chief Executive of IT Governance Limited, the one-stop-shop for books, tools, training and consultancy on IT governance, risk management and compliance.

Alan is an international authority on information security management and on ISO27001 (formerly BS7799), the international security standard. With colleague Steve Watkins he wrote the definitive compliance guide, *IT Governance: An International Guide to Data Security and ISO27001 / ISO27002*, the 5th edition of which was published in 2012. This work is based on his experience of leading the world's first successful implementation of BS7799 (the forerunner of ISO27001) and is the basis for the UK Open University's postgraduate course on information security.

Other books written by Alan include *The Case for ISO27001* and *Nine Steps to Success: An ISO27001:2013 Implementation Overview*, as well as books on corporate governance and IT governance, and several pocket guides in this series.

Alan is a frequent media commentator on information security and IT governance issues, and has contributed articles and expert comment to a wide range of trade, national and online news outlets.

ACKNOWLEDGEMENTS

Copyright in these two information security standards, copies of which can – and should – be purchased from national standards bodies or from _www.itgovernance.co.uk/standards.aspx_, is owned by their publishers. This pocket guide is not a substitute for acquiring and reading the standards themselves and every reader of this pocket guide should obtain copies for themselves.

This pocket guide contains many references to, and summaries of, material that is more comprehensively available in the published standards; it is intended to be a handy reference tool that contains in one place some of the key information that those dealing with the standards and related issues might need. It does not contain enough information for anyone to implement, or audit implementation of, a management system based on either of these standards. It is also a pocket guide to, not a comprehensive manual[1] on, implementing ISO27001.

---

[1] If you are looking for a comprehensive ISO27001 implementation manual, one is available at _www.itgovernance.co.uk/shop/p-772.aspx_.

CONTENTS

INTRODUCTION

It is a truism to say that information is the currency of the information age. Information is, in many cases, the most valuable asset possessed by an organisation, even if that information has not been subject to a formal and comprehensive valuation.

IT governance is the discipline that deals with the structures, standards and processes that boards and management teams apply in order to effectively manage, protect and exploit their organisation's information assets.

Information security management is the subset of IT governance that focuses on protecting and securing an organisation's information assets.

Risks to information assets

An asset can be defined as 'anything that has value to an organisation'. Information assets are subject to a wide range of threats, both external and internal, ranging from the random to the highly specific. Risks include acts of nature, fraud and other criminal activity, user error and system failure.

Information Security Management System

An Information Security Management System (ISMS) is defined (in ISO/IEC 27000) as '*part of the overall management system, based on a business risk approach, to establish, implement, operate, monitor, review, maintain and improve information security. The management system includes organisational structure, policies, planning activities, responsibilities, practices, procedures, processes and resources'.*

CHAPTER 1: THE ISO/IEC 27000 FAMILY OF INFORMATION SECURITY STANDARDS

ISO27001, the international Information Security Management Standard, was published in 2005 and updated in 2013. It is becoming widely known and followed.

It is now part of a much larger family, of which ISO/IEC 27000 is the root for a whole numbered series of international standards for the management of information security.

Developed by a subcommittee of a joint technical committee (ISO/IEC JTC SC27) of the International Standards Organisation (ISO) in Geneva and the International Electrotechnical Commission (IEC), these standards now provide a globally recognised framework for best practice information security management.

The correct designation for most of these standards includes the ISO/IEC prefix and all of them should include a suffix which is their date of publication. Most of these standards, however, tend to be spoken of in shorthand. ISO/IEC 27001:2013, for instance, is often referred to simply as ISO27001.

The first of the ISO27000 series of information security standards has already been published.

ISO/IEC 27001:2013 (ISO27001)

This is the current version of the international standard specification for an Information Security Management System. It is vendor-neutral and technology-independent. It is 'intended to be applicable to all organisations, regardless of type, size or nature'[1] and in every sector (e.g. commercial enterprises, government agencies, not-for-profit organisations), anywhere in the world. It is a management system, not a technology specification, with the formal title 'Information technology – Security techniques – Information security management systems – Requirements'.

ISO/IEC 27002:2013 (ISO27002)

This standard is titled 'Information technology – Security techniques – Code of practice for information security management'. The first edition was published in July 2005, having been initially and originally numbered ISO/IEC 17799. The latest edition was published in October 2013.

ISO/IEC 27003

This standard is titled 'Information Technology – Security techniques – Information security management system implementation guidance'. It was published in January 2010.

---

[1] ISO/IEC 27001:2013, Scope 1.

ISO/IEC 27004

ISO/IEC 27004 is titled 'Information technology – Security techniques – Information security management – Measurement'. This Standard is designed to help organisations more effectively address the requirement, contained in Clauses 9.1 to 9.3 of ISO27001, to measure the effectiveness of controls. It was published in December 2009.

ISO/IEC 27005:2011

Information security risk management (based on and incorporating ISO/IEC 13335 MICTS Part 2) was published in June 2008, with a newer edition published in 2011.

ISO/IEC 27006:2011

This standard sets out the requirements for bodies providing audit and certification of information security management systems.

Definitions

The definitions used in all these standards are intended to be consistent with one another and also to be consistent with those used in ISO/IEC Guide 73:2009. ISO/IEC 27000:2012 is also available; it is titled 'Information technology – Security techniques – Information security management systems – Overview and vocabulary'.

CHAPTER 2: BACKGROUND TO THE STANDARDS

The very first formal information security Standard, BS7799, was originally issued in the UK in April 1999 as a two-part standard. An earlier code of practice had been substantially revised and became Part 1 of the new Standard (BS7799-1:1999) and a new Part 2 (BS7799-2:1999) was drafted and added.

The link between the two standards was created at this point:

- Part 1 was a code of practice
- Part 2 was a specification for an ISMS that deployed controls selected from the code of practice.

The original Part 2 specified, in the main body of the Standard, the same set of controls that were described in far greater detail (particularly with regard to implementation) in Part 1. These controls were later removed from the main body of Part 2 and listed in an annex, Annex A.

This relationship continues today, between the specification for the ISMS that is contained in one standard, and the detailed guidance on the information security controls that should be considered in developing and implementing the ISMS which are contained in the other part of the combined standard.

The International Standards Organisation (ISO) and the International Electrotechnical Commission (IEC)[1] then collaborated to adopt and internationalise BS7799-1 as ISO/IEC 17799:2000 in December 2000. ISO17799 was widely used around the world to provide guidance on best-practice information security controls.

ISO 17799 was substantially revised, improved and updated five years later (in 2005) and it was also renumbered into the ISO27000 series.

BS7799-2

BS7799-2:1999 was revised and reissued as BS7799-2:2002. Significant changes occurred at this time, including:

- the alignment of the clause numbering in both parts of the Standard

- the addition of the PDCA model (see *Chapter 15*) to the Standard

- the addition of a requirement to continuously improve the ISMS

- the alignment of the Standard, and its detailed clauses, with ISO9001:2000 and ISO14001:1996,

---

[1] The IEC is 'the leading global organisation that prepares and publishes international standards for all electrical, electronic and related technologies'. Its website is at *www.iec.ch*. The ISO and the IEC work together, within the World Trade Organisation (WTO) framework, to provide technical support for the growth of global markets and to ensure that technical regulations, voluntary standards and conformity assessment procedures do not create unnecessary obstacles to trade. The joint ISO/IEC information centre has a website at *www.standardsinfo.net*.

to facilitate the development of integrated management systems.

ISO27001:2005

Although a number of countries adopted BS7799-2, it was still only a British Standard in June 2005, when ISO/IEC 17799:2005 was to be issued. The decision was taken, at that time, to put BS7799-2 on the 'fast track' to internationalisation and FDIS (Final Draft International Standard) was issued in June 2005. BS7799-2:2005 (ISO/IEC 27001:2005) was finally published in October 2005.

ISO27001:2013

Following an extended consultation with member organisations of the ISO/IEC, the latest edition of ISO27001 was released in October 2013. It shifted the focus towards creating an ISMS that complements the organisation and its processes, and reduced redundancy within the specification and controls.

Correspondence between ISO27001 and ISO27002

Annex A to ISO/IEC 27001:2013 lists the 114 controls that are in ISO/IEC 27002:2013, follows the same numbering system and uses the same words for the controls and control objectives.

The preface to the Annex states: 'The control objectives and controls [referred to in this edition] are directly derived from and aligned with those listed in ISO/IEC 27002:2013.' ISO/IEC 27001 requires that the organisation 'determine all controls that are necessary to implement the information security risk treatment option(s) chosen'[2].

ISO27002 also provides substantial implementation guidance on how individual controls should be approached. Anyone implementing an ISO27001 ISMS will need to acquire and study copies of both ISO27001 and ISO27002.

While ISO27001 in effect mandates the use of ISO27002 as a source of guidance on controls, control selection and control implementation, it does not limit the organisation's choice of controls. The specification states: 'The control objectives and controls listed in Annex A are not exhaustive and additional control objectives and controls may be needed.'[3]

Use of the Standards

Both standards recognise that information security cannot be achieved through technological means alone, and should never be implemented in a way that is either out of line with the organisation's approach to risk or undermines or creates difficulties for its business operations.

Effective information security is defined in ISO27000 as the 'preservation of confidentiality, integrity and availability of information'.

---

[2] ISO/IEC 27001:2013, 6.1.3 Information security risk treatment.
[3] Ibid.

CHAPTER 3: SPECIFICATION VS CODE OF PRACTICE

ISO/IEC 27001:2013 is a specification for an information security management system. It uses words like '*shall*'. It sets out requirements. It is the specification against which first-, second- and third-party audits can be carried out.

A first-party audit is an audit of an organisation's own practices that is carried out by that organisation. A second-party audit is carried out by a partner organisation, usually pursuant to a commercial relationship of some description. A third-party audit is one carried out by an independent third party, such as a certification body or external auditor.

A code of practice or a set of guidelines uses words like '*should*' and '*may*', allowing individual organisations to choose which elements of the standard to implement, and which not. This inbuilt element of choice means that ISO27002 is not capable of providing a firm standard against which an audit can be conducted. ISO27001, however, is prescriptive and does not provide any such latitude.

Any organisation that implements an ISMS which it wishes to have assessed against ISO27001 will have to follow the specification contained in that Standard.

As a general rule, organisations implementing an ISMS based on ISO/IEC 27001:2013 will do well to pay close attention to the wording of the standard itself, and to be aware of any revisions to it. Non-compliance with any official revisions, which usually occur on a three-year and a five-year cycle, will jeopardise an existing certification.

An appropriate first step is to obtain and read a copy of ISO/IEC 27001:2013. Copies can be purchased from the ISO website, from national standards bodies and from *www.itgovernance.co.uk/standards.aspx*. There should be a choice of hard copy and downloadable versions to suit individual needs.

CHAPTER 4: CERTIFICATION PROCESS

ISO27001 provides a specification against which an organisation's ISMS can be independently audited by an accredited certification body. If the ISMS is found to conform to the specification, the organisation can be issued with a formal certificate confirming this.

Certification bodies

Certification is carried out by independent, accredited certification bodies. These are called different things in different countries, including 'registration bodies', 'assessment and registration bodies', 'certification/registration bodies' and 'registrars'. Whatever they are called, they all do the same thing and are subject to the same requirements.

An accredited certification body is one that has demonstrated to a national accreditation body (such as, for example, UKAS – the UK Accreditation Service) that it has fully met the international and any national standards set down for the operation of certification bodies. These standards usually restrict the capacity of an accredited certification body to provide consultancy services in relation to a standard for which it also provides certification services.

Organisations that are seeking independent certification of their ISMS should always go to an accredited certification body. Their certificates are usually valid for three years and are subject to periodic maintenance visits by the certification body; they have international credibility and will be issued in line with an approved system for the issue and maintenance of such certificates. An approved version of the scheme's certification symbol may be used in the organisation's marketing material.

There is a list of some accredited certification and other bodies in the links pages of *www.itgovernance.co.uk/web_links.aspx*.

CHAPTER 5: THE ISMS AND ISO27001

Definition of information security

ISO27000 defines information security (in its definitions section) as the '*preservation of confidentiality, integrity and availability of information; in addition, other properties such as authenticity, accountability, non-repudiation and reliability can also be involved*'.

Information risks can affect one or more of the three fundamental attributes of an information asset – its

- availability
- confidentiality
- integrity.

These three attributes are defined in ISO27000 as follows:

- Availability: '*the property of being accessible and usable upon demand by an authorised entity*', which allows for the possibility that information has to be accessed by software programs as well as human users.

- Confidentiality: '*the property that information is not made available or disclosed to unauthorised individuals, entities, or processes*'.

- Integrity: '*the property of protecting the accuracy and completeness of assets*'.

The ISMS

An ISMS – which the Standard is clear includes 'organisational structure, policies, planning activities, responsibilities, practices, procedures, processes and resources,'[1] – is a structured, coherent management approach to information security, which is designed to ensure the effective interaction of the three key components of implementing an information security policy:

- process (or procedure)
- technology
- user behaviour.

The Standard's requirement is that the design and implementation of an ISMS should be directly influenced by each organisation's 'needs and objectives, security requirements, the organisational processes used and the size and structure of the organisation'.[2]

ISO27001 is not a one-size-fits-all solution, nor was it ever seen as a static, fixed entity that interferes with the growth and development of a business. The Standard explicitly recognises that:

- the ISMS 'will be scaled in accordance with the needs of the organisation', and
- the ISMS is 'expected to change over time'.

---

[1] ISO/IEC 27000:2012, Terms and definitions, 2.34, note.
[2] ISO/IEC 27001:2013, Introduction General, 0.1.

CHAPTER 6: OVERVIEW OF ISO/IEC 27001:2013

The formal title of this Standard is 'Information technology – Security techniques – Information security management systems – Requirements'. From October 2013, it replaced the previous edition, ISO/IEC 27001:2005.

Including end pieces, this Standard is only 30 pages long. The core of the Standard is contained in the nine pages that set out the specifications for the design and implementation of an information security management system, and in the 13 pages of Annex A, which contain the 114 individual controls which must, under the Standard, be considered for applicability.

The ISMS specification is contained in Clauses 4 to 10 of ISO27001.

The Standard's contents (main clauses and annexes) are:

0. Introduction
1. Scope
2. Normative references
3. Terms and definitions
4. Context of the organisation
5. Leadership
6. Planning
7. Support
8. Operation
9. Performance evaluation

10. Improvement

- Annex A: Reference control objectives and controls
- Bibliography

CHAPTER 7: OVERVIEW OF ISO/IEC 27002:2013

This Standard's title is 'Information technology – Security techniques – Code of practice for information security management'. Published in October 2013, it replaced the previous edition, ISO/IEC 27002:2005.

It is a code of practice, not a specification. It uses words like 'should' and 'may': It '*may* be regarded as a starting point for developing organisation-specific guidelines'.[1]

ISO27002 is more than twice as long as ISO27001, with 90 pages, 8 of which are introductory material. Some 78 pages deal, in detail, with information security controls. This standard has 18 clauses, as shown below:

- Foreword
  0. Introduction
  1. Scope
  2. Normative references
  3. Terms and definitions
  4. Structure of this standard
  5. Information security policies
  6. Organisation of information security
  7. Human resource security
  8. Asset management
  9. Access control
  10. Cryptography

---

[1] ISO/IEC 27002:2013, 0.4: Introduction, Developing your own guidelines; added emphasis.

11. Physical and environmental security

12. Operations security

13. Communications security

14. System acquisition, development and maintenance

15. Supplier relationships

16. Information security incident management

17. Information security aspects of business continuity management

18. Compliance

- Bibliography

The 14 clauses numbered from five to eighteen contain the controls that are specified in Annex A of ISO27001. These clauses collectively contain 35 security categories. The numbering of the controls is exactly the same in both Standards. There is no significance to the order of the clauses; 'depending on the circumstances, security controls from any or all clauses could be important'.[2]

The security categories

Each security category contains:

- a control objective, stating what has to be achieved

- one or more controls that can be deployed to achieve that stated objective.

Each control within each security category is laid out in exactly the same way. There is:

---

[2] ISO/IEC 27002:2013, Clause 4.1.

- a control statement, which describes (in the context of the control objective) what the control is for;

- implementation guidance, which is detailed guidance which may (or may not) help individual organisations implement the control;

- other information that needs to be considered, including reference to other standards.

CHAPTER 8: DOCUMENTATION AND RECORDS

One of the key reasons for designing and implementing a management system is to enable the organisation to move beyond what is known, in the terms of the capability maturity model, as an '*ad hoc*' organisation. An *ad hoc* organisation is one that has 'no fixed processes, or procedures, results depend very much on individual performance, and a lot of people's time is spent on "fire fighting", fixing bugs in software, and resolving incidents'.[1]

ISO9001:2008 is a well-known and widely implemented quality assurance or business process management system. If the organisation does not already have an existing ISO9001 certified management system and needs guidance on the documentation and document control covered by Clause 7.5 of ISO27001, then it should obtain and use the guidance in any current manual on the implementation of ISO9001.

Note that the ISO27001 specifications for document control (7.5.3) reflect those contained in ISO9001:2008, where they are numbered 4.2.3 and 4.2.4 respectively.

Document control requirements

ISO27001 explicitly requires the management system to be documented. Control A.12.1.1 explicitly requires security procedures to be documented, maintained and made available to all users who need them. Other

---

[1] *IT Service CMM: A Pocket Guide*, Van Haren, 2004, page 24.

explicit
documentation requirements in Annex A include:

- A.5.1.1: policies for information security;
- A.6.1.1: documented roles and responsibilities for human resources security;
- A.8.1.3: acceptable use of assets;
- A.9.1.1: access control policy;
- A.18.1.1: identification of applicable legislation.

Many of the other controls require 'formal' procedures or 'clear' communication; while these could technically be achieved without being documented, the expectation is that all processes and procedures will be.

Contents of the ISMS documentation

Documentation has to be complete, comprehensive, in line with the requirements of the Standard and tailored to suit the needs of individual organisations. The ISMS must be fully documented. ISO27001 describes the minimum documentation that should be included in the ISMS.

Not every organisation has to implement an equally complex documentation structure. The Standard notes that 'the extent of documented information for an [ISMS] can differ from one organisation to another due to […] the size of the organisation and its type of activities and their interactions'.[2]

---

[2] ISO/IEC 27001:2013, 7.5.1, General, note b.

With the release of ISO 27001:2013, there is no longer a distinction between documents and records, and both are subject to the same requirements. Regardless, organisations may find it useful to maintain this distinction, especially if an ISO9001 Quality Management System (QMS) is in place, as this does maintain the distinction.

There are specific records that the organisation has to keep in the ordinary course of its business and these will be subject to a variety of legislative and regulatory retention periods. Records that provide evidence of the effectiveness of the ISMS are of a different nature from those records that the ISMS exists to protect, but, nevertheless, these records must themselves be controlled and must remain legible, readily identifiable and retrievable. This means that, particularly for electronic records, a means of accessing them must be retained even after hardware and software has been upgraded.

Annex A document controls

There are further document-related controls in Annex A that should be included in the document control aspects of the ISMS. They are all important controls in their own right. These controls are:

- A.8.2.1: classification of information, which deals with confidentiality levels

- A.8.2.2: labelling of information, which deals with how confidentiality levels are marked on information and information media

- A.8.2.3: handling of assets, which deals with procedures for handling assets in accordance with their classification

- A.18.1.3: protection of records, which deals with document retention

- A.18.1.4: privacy and protection of personally identifiable information, which deals with the confidentiality of personal information.

CHAPTER 9: MANAGEMENT RESPONSIBILITY

Implementation of an ISMS is something that ISO27001 recognises will affect the whole organisation. The requirements around scoping and the information security policy are explicit that there needs to be a documented justification for any exclusion from the scope, and that the policy should apply across the organisation.

ISO27001 is also clear that the ISMS should be designed to meet the needs of the organisation, and should be implemented and managed in a way that meets – and continues to meet – those needs.

Management direction

ISO27001 contains a requirement that management should '[communicate] the importance of effective information security management and of conforming to the information security management system requirements'.[1] These requirements have grown stronger in successive versions of the ISMS Standard as it has become ever clearer that designing and establishing an ISMS is difficult without such management support and direction.

The strategic nature of an ISMS is explicitly recognised in Clause 4.4 of the Standard, which states the requirement that the organisation 'shall establish, implement, maintain and continually improve an information security management system'. This strategic

---

[1] ISO/IEC 27001:2013, 5.1.d.

position is established (in Clause 4.1) as being founded on an understanding of the organisation and its context.

Management's responsibility is so important that Clause 5 is devoted to setting out in detail the management requirements. These requirements are that management 'shall demonstrate leadership and commitment with respect to the information security management system', 'shall establish an information security policy', and 'shall ensure that the responsibilities and authorities for roles relevant to information security are assigned and communicated'.

Management-related controls

There are a number of controls in Annex A that specify management involvement and are linked to Section 5 of ISO27001. These, numbered as they appear in Annex A, are as follows:

- A.5.1.1: policies for information security

- A.6.1.2: segregation of duties

- A.9.2.5: review of user access rights

- A.18.2.2: compliance with security policies and standards.

Requirement for management review

In addition to the control requirements, the Standard mandates, at Clause 9.3 (management review), that management, at planned intervals, must 'review the organisation's ISMS [...] to ensure its continuing suitability, adequacy and effectiveness'.[2] This section defines clearly the required input to the review process; it includes the output from the organisation's monitoring and review activity.

The output from the management review should be documented, and should also be implemented; it should lead to steady, ongoing and continuous improvement of the ISMS. An ISO27001-certificated ISMS will be subject to regular certification reviews during the currency of the certificate; these reviews will focus on how the organisation and its management have driven the continuous improvement process.

---

[2] ISO/IEC 27001:2013.

CHAPTER 10: PROCESS APPROACH AND THE PDCA CYCLE

The PDCA model or cycle is the Plan–Do–Check–Act cycle that was originated in the 1950s by W. Edwards Deming. It states that that business processes should be treated as though they are in a continuous feedback loop so that managers can identify and change those parts of the process that need improvement. The process, or an improvement to the process, should first be planned, then implemented and its performance measured, then the measurements should be checked against the planned specification, and any deviations or potential improvements identified and reported to management for a decision about what action to take.

PDCA and ISO27001

In the previous edition of ISO27001, Clause 0.2 clearly stated that the process required for implementing an ISMS was PDCA. With the release of ISO27001:2013, however, this is no longer a mandatory feature of the ISMS. In fact, ISO27001:2013 offers no explicit guidance with regard to the continual improvement approach, other than specifying that one is required, allowing the organisation to identify its own best practice for its ISMS.

Despite the removal of the PDCA cycle from the specification, it remains a valid and effective process for implementing the ISMS. In the absence of a defined process, it is sensible to apply PDCA, which has been a practical approach for many years.

Application of the PDCA cycle to a process approach means that, following the basic principles of process design, there needs to be both inputs to and outputs from the process. An ISMS takes as its input the information security requirements and expectations of the interested parties and, through the necessary actions and processes, produces information security outcomes that meet those requirements and expectations.[1]

The PDCA cycle and the clauses of ISO27001

The correspondence between the PDCA cycle and the stages identified in the Standard for the development of the ISMS are as set out below.

Plan (establish the ISMS):

- define the organisation and its context (Clause 4.1)

- define the scope of the ISMS (Clause 4.3)

- define the information security policy (Clause 5.2)

- define a systematic approach to risk assessment (Clause 6.1.2)

- carry out a risk assessment to identify, within the context of the policy and ISMS scope, the important information assets of the organisation and the risks to them (Clause 8.2)

- assess the risks (Clause 6.1.2.d)

---

[1] ISO/IEC 27001:2013, 4.2 and 4.3.

- identify and evaluate options for the treatment of these risks (Clause 6.1.3)

- select, for each risk treatment decision, the control objectives and controls to be implemented (Clause 6.1.3.b)

- prepare a statement of applicability (SoA). (Clause 6.1.3.d).

Do (implement and operate the ISMS):

- formulate the risk treatment plan and its documentation, including planned processes and detailed procedures (Clause 6.1.3.e)

- implement the risk treatment plan and planned controls (Clause 8.3)

- provide appropriate training for affected staff, as well as awareness programmes (Clause 7.2)

- manage operations and resources in line with the ISMS (Clauses 7.2 and 8.1)

- implement procedures that enable prompt detection of, and response to, security incidents. (Clause 8.1).

Check (monitor and review the ISMS):

- the 'check' stage has, essentially, only one step (or set of steps): monitoring, reviewing, testing and audit (Clause 9)

- monitoring, reviewing, testing and audit is an ongoing process that has to cover the whole system.

Act (maintain and improve the ISMS):

- testing and audit outcomes should be reviewed by management, as should the ISMS in the light of the changing risk environment, technology or other circumstances; improvements to the ISMS should be identified, documented and implemented (Clause 9)

- thereafter, it will be subject to ongoing review, further testing and improvement implementation, a process known as 'continuous improvement'. (Clause 10).

CHAPTER 11: CONTEXT, POLICY AND SCOPE

The first planning step is the scoping exercise.

The scoping requirement is contained in Clause 4.3) of ISO27001. The requirement is that the organisation will 'determine the boundaries and applicability of the information security management system to establish its scope [taking into consideration] external and internal issues, the requirements [of interested parties, and] interfaces and dependencies between activities performed by the organisation, and those that are performed by other organisations'.

This is built upon the understanding of the organisation and its context, as well as the expectations of interested parties. Clause 4.1 states that the organisation 'shall determine external and internal issues that are relevant to its purpose and that affect its ability to achieve the intended outcome(s) of its information security management system'. Clause 4.2 requires the organisation to identify interested parties and their requirements with relation to the ISMS. This 'may include legal and regulatory requirements and contractual obligations'.

The scoping exercise

A scoping exercise should determine what is within, and what is outside, the ISMS. The ISMS will, in effect, erect a barrier between everything that is inside its perimeter and everything that is outside it. The development of the ISMS will require every point at which there is contact between the outside and the inside to be treated as a potential risk point, requiring specific and appropriate treatment.

Assets, like processes, cannot be half-in and half-out of the ISMS; they are either wholly in or wholly out.

Legal and regulatory framework

The legal and regulatory framework (4.2) also creates a specific perspective on the scoping of the ISMS. Clearly, information and information management processes that are all within the scope of any one single regulation, or other legal requirement, must all be within the scope of the ISMS.

Policy definition

The second major planning step required by ISO27001 is policy definition.

Clause 5.2 requires the organisation to define an information security policy. This requirement is also contained in the first control in Annex A, control number 5.1.1. This is the first of many clauses in ISO27001 that are supported by the guidance and best practice of ISO27002. Clause 5.1.1 of ISO27002 expands on the similarly numbered Annex A requirement and matches the specification contained in Clause 5.2 of ISO27001. The control objective served by the issue of a policy document is that it provides 'management direction and support for information security in accordance with business requirements and relevant laws and regulation.'[1]

---

[1] ISO/IEC 27002:2013, 5.1.

Policy and business objectives

Clause 5.1.1 goes on to state that the policy document should set out 'the organisation's approach to managing its information security objectives'. The Standard's perspective is that a successful and useful ISMS will be one that does not undermine or block business activity. The significant risk in implementing systems that block business activity, that are not in line with business objectives, is that people inside the business will ignore or bypass the ISMS controls.

The information security policy must be signed off by senior management and made available as appropriate to anyone who needs it.

CHAPTER 12: RISK ASSESSMENT

The next planning step is the information security risk assessment. Risk assessment is dealt with in clauses 6.1.2 and 8.2 of ISO27001, supported by the guidance of ISO27002 Clause 0.2.

Rather than being immediately complementary, ISO27002 recognises the value of additional control and management frameworks. The risk assessment guidance offered in ISO27002, therefore, is necessarily brief as it encourages the organisation to choose the approach which is most applicable to its industry, complexity and risk environment.

Link to ISO/IEC 27005

ISO27005 is a code of practice and provides detailed and extensive guidance on how to implement the requirements mandated by ISO27001. While the risk assessment must be carried out in line with the requirements of ISO27001, the guidance of ISO27005 can be drawn on in developing the detailed risk assessment methodology.

Objectives of risk treatment plans

Risk treatment plans have four linked objectives. These are to

- eliminate risks (terminate them),
- reduce those that cannot be eliminated to 'acceptable' levels (treat them),

- tolerate them, exercising carefully the controls that keep them 'acceptable', or

- transfer them, by means of contract or insurance, to some other organisation.

ISO27001 requires the organisation (in Clause 6.1.2) to define the risk acceptance criteria and the criteria for performing information security risk assessments. The process adopted by management to make these decisions must be 'tailored to the needs of the organisation'.[1] Furthermore, whatever risk assessment process the organisation chooses to implement, it must be able to 'produce consistent, valid and comparable results'.[2]

A risk treatment plan can only be drawn up once the risks have been identified, analysed and assessed. The risk assessment process should be designed to operate within the organisation's overall risk treatment framework (if there is one) and should follow the specific requirements of ISO27001.

Legal, regulatory and contractual requirements

ISO27001 requires the organisation to implement any controls that might be necessary to meet its legal, regulatory and contractual obligations. Once these controls have been selected and implemented, the organisation can proceed to carry out a risk assessment to identify what additional controls might be required in order for it to manage risks within its risk tolerance level.

---

[1] ISO/IEC 27001:2013, 1.
[2] ISO/IEC 27001:2013, 6.1.2.b.

Risk assessment process

ISO27001 sets out seven steps that must be followed in carrying out a risk assessment:

- identify risks associated with the loss of confidentiality, availability and integrity of information within the scope of the ISMS;

- identify the risk owners;

- assess the consequences that may result if an identified risk materialises;

- assess the likelihood of that risk occurring;

- determine the levels of risk;

- compare the results of the analysis against the risk criteria;

- prioritise the risks for treatment.

Identify risks (6.1.2.c.1)

Information security risks are 'the potential that *threats* will exploit *vulnerabilities* of an information asset or group of information assets and thereby cause harm to an organisation.'[3]

Threats

Threats are things that can go wrong or that can 'attack' the identified assets. They can be either external or internal. ISO27001 requires the ISMS to be based on the foundation of a detailed identification and assessment of

---

[3] ISO/IEC 27000, 2.61, Note 6; emphasis added.

the threats to each individual information asset that is within the scope. Threats will vary according to the industry and the scope of the ISMS.

Vulnerabilities

These leave a system open to attack by something that is classified as a threat, or allow an attack to have some success or greater impact. A vulnerability can be exploited by a threat. Identify – for every identified asset and for each of the threats listed alongside each of the assets – the vulnerabilities that each threat could exploit.

Identify risk owners (6.1.2.c.2)

In addition to the asset owners that must be identified in the asset register prior to the risk assessment, each risk identified is assigned an owner. It is important to recognise the distinction in roles between the asset owner and the risk owner. While the asset owner is responsible for ensuring that the asset is inventoried, classified and protected, controlled and properly handled[4], the risk owner has no specific responsibilities towards the asset, but is responsible for managing the risk and accepting residual information security risks. It is also important to note that a single risk may affect several assets.

Assess the consequences of the risk (6.1.2.d.1)

The successful exploitation of a vulnerability by a threat will have an impact on the asset's availability, confidentiality or integrity. These impacts should all be

---

[4] ISO/IEC 27002, 8.1.2.

identified and, wherever possible, assigned a value. ISO27001 is clear that these impacts should be assessed under each of these three headings; a single threat, therefore, could exploit more than one vulnerability and each exploitation could have more than one type of impact.

The Standard's requirement is to assess the extent of the possible loss to the business for each potential impact. One object of this exercise is to prioritise treatment (controls) and to do so in the context of the organisation's acceptable risk threshold; it is acceptable to categorise possible loss rather than attempt to calculate it exactly.

Likelihood (6.1.2.d.2)

There must be an assessment of the likelihood or probability of the identified impact actually occurring. Probabilities might range from 'not very likely' (e.g. major earthquake in southern England destroying primary and backup facilities) to 'almost daily' (e.g. several thousand automated malware and hack attacks against the network).

Levels of risk (6.1.2.d.3)

Assess the risk level for each impact as a combination of the consequences and the likelihood. Every organisation has to decide for itself what it wants to set as the thresholds for categorising each potential impact.

Comparing the risk analysis with the risk criteria (6.1.2.e.1)

Take the levels of risk established during the analysis and compare them with the risk criteria established at the start of the process. This provides a broader overview of the level of overall risk facing the organisation on a risk-by-risk and asset-by-asset basis, and provides the basis of the rest of the ISMS.

Prioritise the risks (6.1.2.e.2)

The further a risk deviates from the risk acceptance criteria, the higher its priority. Even in the event that a risk falls within the acceptance criteria, it may be valuable to assign it a priority for eventual treatment, or it may be predicted that the risk will increase under specific circumstances.

Risk treatment plan

Clause 6.1.3 of ISO27001 requires the organisation to formulate a risk treatment plan. This should identify the appropriate management action, responsibilities and priorities for managing information security risks. The risk treatment plan must be documented. It should be set within the context of the organisation's information security policy and it should clearly identify the organisation's approach to risk and its criteria for accepting risk. These criteria should, where a risk treatment framework already exists, be consistent with the requirements of ISO27001.

CHAPTER 13: THE STATEMENT OF APPLICABILITY (SOA)

While the statement of applicability is central to an ISMS and to accredited certification of the ISMS (it is the document from which an auditor will begin the process of confirming whether or not appropriate controls are in place and operative), it can really only be prepared once the risk assessment has been completed and the risk treatment plan documented.

The statement of applicability is a statement as to which of the controls identified in Annex A to ISO27001 are applicable to the organisation, and which are not. It can also contain additional controls selected from other sources.

SoA and external parties

The SoA must be reviewed on a defined, regular basis. It is the document that is used to demonstrate to third parties the degree of security that has been implemented and is usually referred to, with its issue status, in the certificate of compliance issued by third-party certification bodies.

Controls and Annex A

Clause 6.1.3.b requires the organisation to determine all controls necessary to implement the risk treatment plan. Significantly, this is completed *before* consulting Annex A.

Clause 6.1.3.c of ISO27001 requires the organisation to select appropriate control objectives and controls from those specified in Annex A to match the controls selected in 6.1.3.b. However, it states that additional controls may also be selected from other sources. As part of composing the SoA in 6.1.3.d, the organisation is required to justify the selection (and exclusion) of controls.

ISO27002 provides good practice on the purpose and implementation of each of the controls listed in Annex A. There are, however, some areas in which organisations may need to go further than is specified in ISO27002; the extent to which this may be necessary is driven by the degree to which technology and threats have evolved since the finalisation of ISO27002.

Controls (6.1.3.b)

Controls are the countermeasures for vulnerabilities. The formal ISO27000 definition of a control is a 'means of managing risk, including policies, procedures, guidelines, practices or organisational structures, which can be of administrative, technical, management, or legal nature. Control is also used as a synonym for safeguard or countermeasure'.[1]

Apart from knowingly accepting risks that fall within whatever criteria of acceptability the organisation has adopted in its risk treatment plan, or transferring the risk (through contract or insurance), the organisation can decide to implement a control to reduce the risk.

---

[1] ISO/IEC 27000, 2.16.

Residual risks

It is not possible or practical to provide total security against every single risk, but it is possible to provide effective security against most risks by controlling them to a level where the residual risk is acceptable to management. The risk owner must formally accept the residual risk (Clause 6.1.3.f).

Risks can and do change, however, so the process of reviewing and assessing risks and controls is an essential, ongoing one (Clause 8.2).

Control objectives

Controls are selected in the light of a control objective. A control objective is a statement of an organisation's intent to control some part of its processes or assets and what it intends to achieve through application of the control. One control objective may be served by a number of controls.

Annex A of ISO27001 identifies appropriate control objectives and lists controls for each of them, which at a minimum serve those objectives. The organisation must select its control objectives from Annex A in the light of its risk assessment, and then ensure that the controls it chooses to implement (whether from the Annex or from additional sources) will enable it to achieve the identified objective.

Plan for security incidents

It is important that, when considering controls, the likely security incidents that may need to be detected are identified, considered and planned for. The process of selecting individual controls from those listed in the

Standard's Annex A should include consideration of what evidence will be required, and what measurements of effectiveness (6.1.1.e.2) will be made to demonstrate:

- that the control has been implemented and is working effectively

- that each risk has, thereby, been reduced to an acceptable level, as required by Clause 6.1.2.a.1 of the Standard. Controls must be constructed in such a manner that any error, or failure during execution, is capable of prompt detection and that planned corrective action, whether automated or manual, is effective in reducing to an acceptable level the risk of whatever may happen next.

CHAPTER 14: IMPLEMENTATION

Implementation of the ISMS involves the following five tasks:

- Implement the risk treatment plan and the controls identified in the SoA (8.3).

- Define how to measure and assess the effectiveness of all the controls (9.1.b).

- Implement training and awareness programmes (7.2 and 7.3), which links to Control A.7.2.2 – information security awareness, education and training.

- Manage the ISMS (8.1). All the interlocking controls and processes must be kept working, and new threats identified, evaluated and, if necessary, neutralised. People must be recruited and trained, their performance supervised, and their skills developed in line with the changing needs of the business.

- Implement an incident detection and response procedure (10.1), which links to Clause 16 of Annex A, information security incident management. This clause contains seven controls that differentiate between an event and an incident and define how the response should be managed.

CHAPTER 15: CHECK AND ACT

Clause 9 of the Standard is all about monitoring and review. It contains the requirement for management to be actively involved in the long-term management of the ISMS while recognising the reality that the information security threat environment changes even more quickly than the business environment. This clause deals, broadly, with three types of activity: monitoring, auditing and reviewing.

Monitoring

The purpose of monitoring activity is primarily to detect processing errors and information security events quickly so that immediate corrective action can be taken. Monitoring should be formal, systematic and widespread. Security category A.12.4 (logging and monitoring) contains controls that are specifically related to monitoring IT activity and these are linked to this part of ISO27001. Control area A.16, information security incident management, also recognises that the organisation must monitor for deviations and incidents, respond to them and learn from them.

Auditing

Audits should be planned to ensure that the controls documented in the SoA are effective and are being applied, and to identify non-conformances and opportunities for improvement. Control objectives A.18.1 (compliance with legal and contractual requirements) and A.18.2 (information security reviews) deal specifically with this issue and mandate regular, planned compliance reviews at both the process and the technical levels. Control objective A.12.7 (information systems audit considerations) deals with the security requirements for audit tools. The audit requirement is described in more depth in Clause 9.2 of ISO27001, which lays out two important aspects of the process:

- The organisation 'shall plan, establish, implement and maintain an audit programme(s), including the frequency, methods, responsibilities, planning requirements and reporting'.[1]

- The audit programme 'shall take into consideration the importance of the processes concerned and the results of previous audits'.[2]

Management at all levels of the organisation has a role to play in the effective implementation, maintenance and improvement of the ISMS. This must be taken into account in managerial and supervisory job descriptions, employment contracts, induction and other training, and performance reviews.

Reviewing

Reviews of internal and external audit policies, performance reports, exception reports, risk assessment reports and all the associated policies and procedures are undertaken to ensure that the ISMS is continuing to be effective within its changing context.

The Annex A controls that are directly relevant to this stage of the ISMS PDCA cycle are:

---

[1] ISO/IEC 27001:2013, Clause 9.2.c.
[2] Ibid.

- A.5.1.2: review of the policies for information security

- A.9.2.5: review of user access rights

- A.12.4: 'logging and monitoring' itself as a single control objective that is related, obviously, to logging and monitoring, and which contains four controls

- A.14.1: security requirements of information systems, a control objective that in effect deals with monitoring application use and data processing

- A.15.2.1: monitoring and review of supplier services

- A.16.1.6: learning from information security incidents

- A.17.1.3: verify, review and evaluate information security continuity.

- A.18.2.1: independent review of information security.

All these controls must be addressed in this third phase of the ISMS development and implementation. The findings and outcomes of monitoring and reporting activities must be translated into corrective or improvement action and, for the purposes of the ISMS, the audit trail that demonstrates the decision-making process and the implementation of those decisions should be retained in the ISMS records.

Act – maintain and improve the ISMS

This is a short section, and it reflects the relative brevity of the requirements of section 6.1.1.c of ISO27001. This clause sets out the requirement that the organisation plan to achieve continual improvement of the ISMS. It also links to Section 10 of the Standard, whose two clauses (10.1, nonconformity and corrective action; and 10.2, continual improvement) specify the nature and purpose of the activity that must be part and parcel of the daily actions of everyone involved in the day-to-day management of the ISMS.

CHAPTER 16: MANAGEMENT REVIEW

Clause 9.3 of ISO27001 (and Control objective A.18.2), which deals with management review of the ISMS, stresses that the management review should take into account 'feedback on the information security performance, including trends in [...] nonconformities and corrective actions',[1] as well as any changes anywhere or to anything that might affect the ISMS, and recommendations for improvement.

It should be noted that corrective and preventative action should be prioritised on the basis of a risk assessment.[2]

ISO27001 calls, at Control A.18.2.1, for an 'independent review of information security', which should take place at planned intervals (or whenever there have been significant changes), and should be comprehensive ('control objectives, controls, policies, processes, and procedures'). Third-party certification would meet this control requirement.

Assessing and evaluating risks is a core competence required in any organisation that is serious about achieving and maintaining ISO27001 accredited certification. It is useful to recall the point that the prevention of non-conformities is often more cost-effective than corrective action, which sums up the risk-based, cost-effective, common-sense approach of the Standard.

---

[1] ISO/IEC 27001:2013, 9.3.c.1.
[2] ISO/IEC 27001:2013, 6.1.2.e.2.

CHAPTER 17: ISO27001 ANNEX A

ISO/IEC 27001:2013 Annex A has 14 major clauses or control areas numbered from A.5 to A.18, each of which identifies one or more control objectives. Each control objective is served by one or more controls. Every control is sequentially numbered.

There are, in total, 114 subclauses, each of which has an alphanumeric clause number.

Annex A is aligned with ISO27002; this means that precisely the same control objectives, controls, clause numbering and wording are used in both Annex A and in ISO27002. Note the clear statement that 'the control objectives and controls listed in Annex A are not exhaustive and additional control objectives and controls may be needed'.[1] The 14 control clauses of Annex A (it does not have Clauses 1–4) all start with an A and are listed below.

- A5: Information security policies
- A6: Organisation of information security
- A7: Human resource security
- A8: Asset management
- A9: Access control
- A10: Cryptography
- A11: Physical and environmental security

---

[1] ISO/IEC 27001:2013, 6.1.3.c, Note 2.

- A12: Operations security

- A13: Communications security

- A14: System acquisition, development and maintenance

- A15: Supplier relationships

- A16: Information security incident management

- A17: Information security aspects of business continuity management

- A18: Compliance.

Annex A control areas and controls

Each of the clauses of Annex A deals with one or more security categories, and each security category has a control objective and one or more controls that will serve to secure that objective. The clauses, security categories, control objectives and control names are set out below; the detailed control requirements are contained in the Standard, and this should be acquired and studied.

Clause A5: Information security policies

5.1 **Management direction for information security:** to provide management direction and support for information security in accordance with business requirements and relevant laws and regulations

5.1.1 Policies for information security

5.1.2 Review of the policies for information security

Clause A6: Organisation of information security

6.1 **Internal organisation:** to establish a management framework to initiate and control the implementation and operation of information security within the organisation

6.1.1 Information security roles and responsibilities

6.1.2 Segregation of duties

6.1.3 Contact with authorities

6.1.4 Contact with special interest groups

6.1.5 Information security in project management

6.2 **Mobile devices and teleworking:** to ensure the security of teleworking and use of mobile devices

6.2.1 Mobile device policy

6.2.2 Teleworking

Clause A7: Human resource security

7.1 **Prior to employment:** to ensure that employees and contractors understand their responsibilities and are suitable for the roles for which they are considered

7.1.1 Screening

7.1.2 Terms and conditions of employment

7.2 **During employment:** to ensure that employees and contractors are aware of and fulfil their information security responsibilities

7.2.1 Management responsibilities

7.2.2 Information security awareness, education and training

7.2.3 Disciplinary process

7.3 **Termination and change of employment:** to protect the organisation's interests as part of the process of changing or terminating employment

7.3.1 Termination or change of employment responsibilities

Clause A8: Asset management

8.1 **Responsibility for assets:** to identify organisational assets and define appropriate protection responsibilities

8.1.1 Inventory of assets

8.1.2 Ownership of assets

8.1.3 Acceptable use of assets

8.1.4 Return of assets

8.2 **Information classification:** to ensure that information receives an appropriate level of protection in accordance with its importance to the organisation

8.2.1 Classification of information

8.2.2 Labelling of information

8.2.3 Handling of assets

8.3 **Media handling:** to prevent unauthorised disclosure, modification, removal or destruction of information stored on media

8.3.1   Management of removable media

8.3.2   Disposal of media

8.3.3   Physical media transfer

Clause A9: Access control

9.1   **Business requirements of access control:** to limit access to information and information processing
facilities

9.1.1   Access control policy

9.1.2   Access to networks and networking services

9.2   **User access management:** to ensure authorised user access and to prevent unauthorised access to systems and services

9.2.1   User registration and de-registration

9.2.2   User access provisioning

9.2.3   Management of privileged access rights

9.2.4   Management of secret authentication information of users

9.2.5   Review of user access rights

9.2.6   Removal or adjustment of access rights

9.3   **User responsibilities:** to make users accountable for safeguarding their authentication information

9.3.1   Use of secret authentication information

9.4 **System and application access control:** to prevent unauthorised access to systems and applications

9.4.1 Information access restriction

9.4.2 Secure log-on procedures

9.4.3 Password management system

9.4.4 Use of privileged utility programs

9.4.5 Access control to program source code

Clause A10: Cryptography

10.1 **Cryptographic controls:** to ensure proper and effective use of cryptography to protect the confidentiality, authenticity and/or integrity of information

10.1.1 Policy on the use of cryptographic controls

10.1.2 Key management

Clause A11: Physical and environmental security

11.1 **Secure areas:** to prevent unauthorised physical access, damage and interference to the organisation's information and information processing facilities

11.1.1 Physical security perimeter

11.1.2 Physical entry controls

11.1.3 Securing offices, rooms and facilities

11.1.4 Protecting against external and environmental threats

11.1.5 Working in secure areas

11.1.6 Delivery and loading areas

11.2 **Equipment:** to prevent loss, damage, theft or compromise of assets and interruption to the organisation's operations

11.2.1 Equipment siting and protection

11.2.2 Supporting utilities

11.2.3 Cabling security

11.2.4 Equipment maintenance

11.2.5 Removal of assets

11.2.6 Security of equipment and assets off-premises

11.2.7 Secure disposal or re-use of equipment

11.2.8 Unattended user equipment

11.2.9 Clear desk and clear screen policy

Clause A12: Operations security

12.1 **Operational procedures and responsibilities:** to ensure correct and secure operations of information processing facilities

12.1.1 Documented operating procedures

12.1.2 Change management

12.1.3 Capacity management

12.1.4 Separation of development, testing and operational environments

12.2 **Protection from malware:** to ensure that information and information processing facilities are protected against malware

12.2.1 Controls against malware

12.3 **Backup:** to protect against loss of data

12.3.1 Information backup

12.4 **Logging and monitoring:** to record events and generate evidence

12.4.1 Event logging

12.4.2 Protection of log information

12.4.3 Administrator and operator logs

12.4.4 Clock synchronisation

12.5 **Control of operational software:** to ensure the integrity of operational software

12.5.1 Installation of software on operational systems

12.6 **Technical vulnerability management:** to prevent exploitation of technical vulnerabilities

12.6.1 Management of technical vulnerabilities

12.6.2 Restrictions on software installation

12.7 **Information systems audit considerations:** to minimise the impact of audit activities on operational systems

12.7.1 Information systems audit controls

Clause A13: Communications security

13.1 **Network security management:** to ensure the protection of information in networks and its supporting information processing facilities

13.1.1 Network controls

13.1.2 Security of network services

13.1.3 Segregation in networks

13.2 **Information transfer:** to maintain the security of information transferred within an organisation and with any external entity

13.2.1 Information transfer policies and procedures

13.2.2 Agreements on information transfer

13.2.3 Electronic messaging

13.2.4 Confidentiality or non-disclosure agreements

Clause A14: System acquisition, development and maintenance

14.1 **Security requirements of information systems:** to ensure that information security is an integral part of information systems across the entire lifecycle. This also includes the requirements for information systems which provide services over public networks

14.1.1 Information security requirements analysis and specification

14.1.2 Securing application services on public networks

14.1.3 Protecting application services transactions

14.2 **Security in development and support processes:** to ensure that information security is designed and implemented within the development lifecycle of information systems

14.2.1 Secure development policy

14.2.2 System change control procedures

14.2.3 Technical review of applications after operating platform changes

14.2.4 Restrictions on changes to software packages

14.2.5 Secure system engineering principles

14.2.6 Secure development environment

14.2.7 Outsourced development

14.2.8 System security testing

14.2.9 System acceptance testing

14.3 **Test data:** to ensure the protection of data used for testing

14.3.1 Protection of test data

Clause A15: Supplier relationships

15.1 **Information security in supplier relationships:** to ensure protection of the organisation's assets that is accessible by suppliers

15.1.1 Information security policy for supplier relationships

15.1.2 Addressing security within supplier agreements

15.1.3 Information and communication technology supply chain

15.2 **Supplier service delivery management:** to maintain an agreed level of information security and service delivery in line with supplier agreements

15.2.1 Monitoring and review of supplier services

15.2.2 Managing changes to supplier services

Clause A16: Information security incident management

16.1 **Management of information security incidents and improvements:** to ensure a consistent and effective approach to the management of information security incidents, including communication on security events and weaknesses

16.1.1 Responsibilities and procedures

16.1.2 Reporting information security events

16.1.3 Reporting information security weaknesses

16.1.4 Assessment of and decision on information security events

16.1.5 Response to information security incidents

16.1.6 Learning from information security incidents

16.1.7 Collection of evidence

Clause A17: Information security aspects of business continuity management

17.1 **Information security continuity:** information security continuity shall be embedded in the organisation's business continuity management systems

17.1.1 Planning information security continuity

17.1.2 Implementing information security continuity

17.1.3 Verify, review and evaluate information security continuity

17.2 **Redundancies:** to ensure availability of information processing facilities

17.2.1 Availability of information processing facilities

Clause A18: Compliance

18.1 **Compliance with legal and contractual requirements:** to avoid breaches of legal, statutory, regulatory or contractual obligations related to information security and of any security requirements

18.1.1 Identification of applicable legislation and contractual requirements

18.1.2 Intellectual property rights

18.1.3 Protection of records

18.1.4 Privacy and protection of personally identifiable information

18.1.5 Regulation of cryptographic controls

18.2 **Information security reviews:** to ensure that information security is implemented and operated in accordance with the organisational policies and procedures

18.2.1 Independent review of information security

18.2.2 Compliance with security policies and standards

18.2.3 Technical compliance review

ITG RESOURCES

IT Governance Ltd sources, creates and delivers products and services to meet the real-world, evolving IT governance needs of today's organisations, directors, managers and practitioners.

The ITG website (*www.itgovernance.co.uk*) is the international one-stop-shop for corporate and IT governance information, advice, guidance, books, tools, training and consultancy.

www.itgovernance.co.uk/infosec.aspx is the information page on our website for information security resources.

Other Websites

Books and tools published by IT Governance Publishing (ITGP) are available from all business booksellers and are also immediately available from the following websites:

www.itgovernance.eu is our euro-denominated website which ships from Benelux and has a growing range of books in European languages other than English.

www.itgovernanceusa.com is a US$-based website that delivers the full range of IT Governance products to North America, and ships from within the continental US.

www.itgovernance.in provides a selected range of ITGP products specifically for customers in the Indian sub-continent.

www.itgovernance.asia delivers the full range of ITGP publications, serving countries across Asia Pacific. Shipping from Hong Kong, US dollars, Singapore dollars, Hong Kong dollars, New Zealand dollars and Thai baht are all accepted through the website.

Toolkits

ITG's unique range of toolkits includes the IT Governance Framework Toolkit, which contains all the tools and guidance that you will need in order to develop and implement an appropriate IT governance framework for your organisation.

For a free paper on how to use the proprietary Calder-Moir IT Governance Framework, and for a free trial version of the toolkit, see *www.itgovernance.co.uk/calder_moir.aspx*.

There is also a wide range of toolkits to simplify implementation of management systems, such as an ISO/IEC 27001 ISMS or an ISO/IEC 22301 BCMS, and these can all be viewed and purchased online at *www.itgovernance.co.uk*.

Training Services

IT Governance offers an extensive portfolio of training courses designed to educate information security, IT governance, risk management and compliance professionals. Our classroom and online training programmes will help you develop the skills required to deliver best practice and compliance to your organisation. They will also enhance your career by providing you with industry standard certifications and increased peer recognition. Our range of courses offer a structured learning path from Foundation to Advanced level in the key topics of information security, IT governance, business continuity and service management.

ISO/IEC 27001:2013 is the international management standard that helps businesses and organisations throughout the world develop a best-in-class Information Security Management System. Knowledge and experience in implementing and maintaining ISO27001 compliance are considered to be essential to building a successful career in information security. We have the world's first programme of certificated ISO27001 education with Foundation, Lead Implementer, Risk Management and Lead Auditor training courses. Each course is designed to provide delegates with relevant knowledge and skills and an industry-recognised qualification awarded by the International Board for IT Governance Qualifications (IBITGQ).

Full details of all IT Governance training courses can be found at *www.itgovernance.co.uk/training.aspx*.

Professional Services and Consultancy

Your mission to plug critical security gaps will be greatly assisted by IT Governance consultants, who have advised hundreds of information security managers in the adoption of ISO27001 Information Security Management Systems (ISMS).

The organisation's assets, security and data systems, not to mention its reputation, are all in your hands. A major security breach could spell disaster. Timely advice and support from IT governance experts will enable you to identify the threats, assess risks and put in place the necessary controls before there's an incident.

At IT Governance, we understand that information, information security and information technology are always business issues, and not just IT ones. Our consultancy services assist you in managing information security strategies in harmony with business goals, conveying the right messages to your colleagues to support decision-making.

For more information about IT Governance Consultancy, see: *www.itgovernance.co.uk/consulting.aspx*.

Publishing Services

IT Governance Publishing (ITGP) is the world's leading IT-GRC publishing imprint that is wholly owned by IT Governance Ltd.

With books and tools covering all IT governance, risk and compliance frameworks, we are the publisher of choice for authors and distributors alike, producing unique and practical publications of the highest quality, in the latest formats available, which readers will find invaluable.

www.itgovernancepublishing.co.uk is the website dedicated to ITGP enabling both current and future authors, distributors, readers and other interested parties, to have easier access to more information. This allows ITGP website visitors to keep up to date with the latest publications and news.

Newsletter

IT governance is one of the hottest topics in business today, not least because it is also the fastest moving.

You can stay up to date with the latest developments across the whole spectrum of IT governance subject matter, including; risk management, information security, ITIL and IT service management, project governance, compliance and so much more, by subscribing to ITG's core publications and topic alert emails.

Simply visit our subscription centre and select your preferences: *www.itgovernance.co.uk/newsletter.aspx*.

Lightning Source UK Ltd.
Milton Keynes UK
UKOW07f1833270115

245214UK00018B/896/P